T0081155

★ HOCKEY SUPERSTARS ★

P.K. SUBBAN

BY MICHAEL BURGAN

CAPSTONE PRESS
a capstone imprint

Sports Illustrated Kids Hockey Superstars are published by Capstone Press, 1710 Roe Crest Drive, North Mankato, Minnesota 56003. www.capstonepub.com

Library of Congress Cataloging-in-Publication Data
Burgan, Michael.
 P.K. Subban / by Michael Burgan.
   pages cm. — (Sports illustrated kids. Hockey superstars)
 Includes bibliographical references and index.
  ISBN 978-1-4296-9134-5 (library binding)
  ISBN 978-1-4914-9023-5 (paperback)
  ISBN 978-1-4914-7604-8 (eBook PDF)
1. Subban, P. K., 1989—Juvenile literature. 2. Hockey players—Canada—Biography.
I. Title.
 GV848.5.S84B87 2016
 796.962092—dc23
 [B]   2015007193

Editorial Credits
Brenda Haugen, editor; Terri Poburka, designer; Eric Gohl, media researcher;
Tori Abraham, production specialist

Photo Credits
Getty Images: Claus Andersen, 11, Jared Wickerham, 4, 6–7, NHLI/Brian Babineau, 26–27, NHLI/Francois Lacasse, 28, Richard Wolowicz, 9; Newscom: Reuters/John Gress, 25, Reuters/Shaun Best, 12, 18, ZUMA Press/Mark Konezny, 1, 15, ZUMA Press/Steve Russell, 23; Sports Illustrated: Damian Strohmeyer, cover, 20, David E. Klutho, 16, 30–31 (background), 32 (background)
Design Elements: Shutterstock

Source Notes
Page 13, sidebar, line 15: Ken Dryden. "P.K. Subban says 'nothing was going to deter me.'" thestar.com. 30 June 2014. 18 March 2015. www.thestar.com/news/ken_dryden_canada_day/2014/06/30/pk_subban_nothing_was_going_to_deter_me.html
Page 19, line 12: "P.K. Subban Talks Racism and Hockey." YouTube. 2 May 2014. 18 March 2015. www.youtube.com/watch?v=TuADxN3-Zws
Page 19, line 14: Randy Sportak. "Subban doesn't deserve heat." *Toronto Sun*. 20 Jan. 2011. 18 March 2015. www.torontosun.com/sports/myflames/2011/01/20/16968411.html
Page 19, sidebar, line 1: "P.K. Subban Talks Racism and Hockey." www.youtube.com/watch?v=TuADxN3-Zws
Page 29, sidebar, line 5: Chris Hosford. "New Hyundai Hockey Helpers Program Launches, Helps 1,000 Canadian Youth Play Hockey." Hyundai. 4 Sept. 2012. 18 March 2015. www.hyundainews.com/us/es/media/pressreleases/37229

Printed in the United States of America in North Mankato, Minnesota.
032015   008823CGF15

TABLE OF CONTENTS

CHAPTER 1
A STAR SHINES 5

CHAPTER 2
WORKING TOWARD SUCCESS ... 8

CHAPTER 3
THE ROAD TO STARDOM 14

CHAPTER 4
ONE OF THE BEST 22

GLOSSARY 30

READ MORE 31

INTERNET SITES 31

INDEX 32

After scoring a big goal, Subban sometimes drops to one knee and pretends to be shooting a bow and arrow. People call this his archer pose.

CHAPTER 1

A STAR SHINES

No one had to tell P.K. Subban the importance of the game he was about to play. His Montreal Canadiens were starting the second round of the 2014 National Hockey League (NHL) playoffs against their fierce rivals the Boston Bruins. Subban had been the Canadiens' second-leading scorer during the regular season. Now he was ready to show his skills against the Bruins.

The **defenseman** started the scoring for Montreal on a first-period **power play**. Subban flicked in a wrist shot from the **blue line**. The puck sailed past several players and into the net.

After two periods the Canadiens held a 2-0 lead. But Boston came back in the third to score two goals of their own. After Montreal once again took the lead, the Bruins tied the score late in the period. The game headed to overtime.

defenseman—a player who lines up in a defensive zone to prevent opponents from getting open shots on goal

power play—when a team has a one- or two-player advantage because the other team has one or more players in the penalty box

blue line—a line painted on the ice that marks the end of a team's offensive zone

The teams fought through one scoreless overtime period. Subban spent plenty of time on the ice. Aside from his team's goalie, Carey Price, Subban would lead the Canadiens in minutes played for the game. Most important, he was on the ice in the second overtime for the game's deciding moment.

With Montreal on another power play, Subban stood along the Bruins' blue line. He took a pass from Andrei Markov, then put his head down and launched a powerful

slap shot. The puck rocketed past the glove of Boston goaltender Tuukka Rask and into the net.

Montreal went on to win the playoff series in seven games. Subban finished the playoff series with four goals and three assists. Scoring aside, many hockey experts thought Subban was the best player on the ice. He had proven he was a star.

slap shot—the fastest and most forceful shot in the game; a player raises his or her stick and slaps the puck hard toward the goal, putting his or her full power behind it

CHAPTER 2

WORKING TOWARD SUCCESS

Many Canadian NHL players come from families with strong hockey traditions. Some can trace their families' hockey-playing history back for decades. P.K. Subban's background is a little different. His father, Karl, came with his family to Sudbury, Ontario, from Jamaica when he was 11 years old. Karl fell in love with hockey, but he struggled to play it. His family didn't have the money to buy him new equipment or pay for him to join teams that played indoors. Karl had to wear used skates and play on outdoor rinks.

As an adult Karl made a decision. He would do all he could to give his children the opportunities he never had. In 1989 he and his wife, Maria, had their first son, Pernell Karl Subban—P.K. for short. P.K. was watching hockey on TV and learning to play the game by the time he was 4 years old. Karl soon saw P.K.'s talent and wanted him to be on the ice as much as possible.

P.K. hugs his father, Karl, after an international tournament in Canada.

Karl was a school vice principal and often worked late. But when he got home, he would wake up P.K. and take him to a nearby rink in their hometown of Toronto, Ontario. Starting at age 6, P.K. sometimes practiced until 2 a.m.! Karl also built an ice rink in the back yard so P.K. and his younger brothers, Malcolm and Jordan, could practice.

P.K. joined the Markham Islanders of the Greater Toronto Hockey League when he was 15. The next year the Belleville Bulls of the much larger Ontario Hockey League (OHL) **drafted** him. The OHL is one of three leagues in Canada for the best young players. As a **rookie** P.K. was not expected to play. But he worked hard and made the team. The next season he was defending against the other teams' top players. He also showed his **offensive** talent with 15 goals and 41 assists. Defensemen are not expected to score often, but offense was a big part of P.K.'s game.

draft—to choose a person to join a sports organization or team

rookie—a first-year player

offense—the team that is in control of the puck and is trying to score

FAST FACT

While growing up P.K. often watched a video of Bobby Orr, one of hockey's greatest defensemen and a great scorer. Orr's play inspired P.K. to always try to be the best player on the ice.

Teammates P.K. Subban and John Tavares celebrate after winning the 2009 U-20 World Junior Hockey Championship.

P.K. was drafted by the Montreal Canadiens in 2007. The news brought tears of joy to Karl Subban because he had always rooted for the Canadiens. P.K., though, would continue to play for Belleville through the 2008–09 season to keep improving his game. He also played for Canada's under-20 national juniors team. The team won two world championships with P.K. on the blue line. During the 2009

THE BEST TEAM EVER

The Montreal Canadiens have a special place in NHL history. Montreal is the largest city in Quebec, a part of Canada where most people speak French. In a hockey-loving region, fans are devoted to the Canadiens. The team has won 24 **Stanley Cups**, more than any other NHL team. Subban knows the Canadiens' amazing history. "This is the greatest organization in hockey," he said. "I want to keep the **legacy** going."

tournament, P.K. scored nine **points** in six games. He was ready to take another step toward playing in the NHL.

Stanley Cup—the trophy given each year to the NHL champion

legacy—qualities and actions a person or team is remembered for

points—a player's total number of goals and assists

CHAPTER 3

THE ROAD TO STARDOM

As the 2009–10 season began, Subban was playing for the Hamilton Bulldogs of American Hockey League (AHL). The AHL is just one step below the NHL. Subban improved his defensive skills while still showing his scoring talents with Hamilton. He notched 53 points during the regular season and added 10 more during the AHL playoffs. One of them was a goal in double overtime that gave the Bulldogs a 5-4 playoff win against the Manitoba Moose. Subban made the league's All-Star Team. He also won the President's Award, which honors a player's outstanding accomplishments during the season.

But the biggest achievement for Subban that year was playing in the NHL for the first time. In February 2010 the Canadiens used him in two games. He notched an assist in each game. The team sent Subban back to Hamilton to continue to develop. But in April Subban was once again in a Canadiens' uniform.

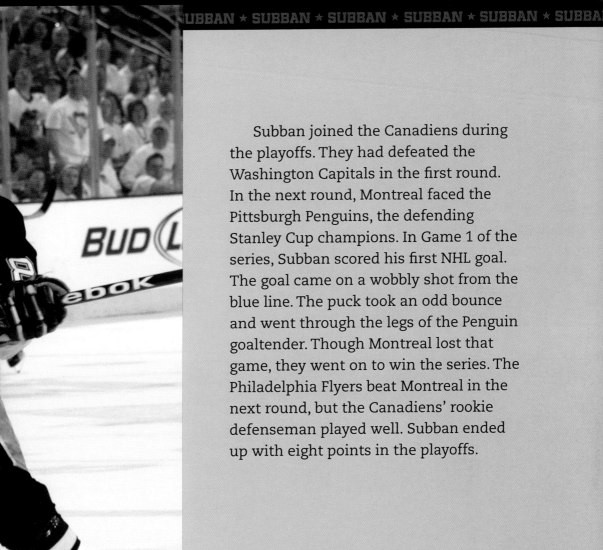

Subban joined the Canadiens during the playoffs. They had defeated the Washington Capitals in the first round. In the next round, Montreal faced the Pittsburgh Penguins, the defending Stanley Cup champions. In Game 1 of the series, Subban scored his first NHL goal. The goal came on a wobbly shot from the blue line. The puck took an odd bounce and went through the legs of the Penguin goaltender. Though Montreal lost that game, they went on to win the series. The Philadelphia Flyers beat Montreal in the next round, but the Canadiens' rookie defenseman played well. Subban ended up with eight points in the playoffs.

FAST FACT

In Game 3 against the Flyers, Subban assisted on three Montreal goals. Only two other Canadiens rookie defensemen had achieved that feat.

Subban strikes his archer pose after scoring his game-winning overtime goal against Calgary in 2011.

RACISM IN THE NHL

Some sportswriters have suggested that P.K. Subban is criticized more than other players because he's black. Almost all NHL players and most fans are white, and racism remains an issue across North America. Subban has experienced this firsthand. Some white fans have made racist remarks to him or called him names online. Subban tries to ignore the comments.

When the 2010–11 season began, there was no doubt that Subban was ready for the NHL. At times, though, it seemed some hockey players and experts were not ready for him.

Subban had always believed strongly in his own talents. Some opponents thought his self-confidence was **arrogance**. Subban also liked to chatter at opposing players to try to irritate them and get them off their game Many **veteran** NHL players expected rookies to be quiet and just play.

Subban scored a game-winning overtime goal against the Calgary Flames in January 2011. He celebrated with his archer move. Some past and present players thought he was showing off. "There's a way to present yourself to other players in the league … hopefully he'll learn," said former Canadiens player Craig Rivet. After the game Subban said, "I should have just celebrated with my teammates."

racism—the belief that one race is better than others

arrogance—exaggerating one's own self worth or importance, often in an overbearing manner

veteran—a longtime player

"Hockey's filled with great people," he said when discussing racism in hockey. "And it's a great sport. And I encourage a lot of people to play it because of the relationships that you make in hockey. Those are the things I would rather talk about than all those other things…." He said he hopes to be a role model for kids of all races who want to play hockey.

But if Subban irritated some players, he proved his skills on the ice. He finished the regular season with 14 goals and 24 assists. One of the highlights came in March against the Minnesota Wild. Subban scored three goals in an 8-1 win. It was the first time a Canadiens' rookie defenseman had scored a **hat trick**.

Perhaps his biggest goal came the next month against the Chicago Blackhawks. With the game tied at 1 in overtime, Subban scored on a slap shot. The goal won the game and guaranteed Montreal a spot in the playoffs.

The Canadiens lost their opening playoff series to the Boston Bruins in seven games. Subban finished with four points. In the 2011–12 season, Subban scored only seven goals, but he racked up 36 points. The next year, though, Subban emerged as a superstar.

hat trick—when a player scores three goals in one game

FAST FACT

Subban was named to the 2010–11 NHL All-Rookie Team.

CHAPTER 4

ONE OF THE BEST

At just 23 years old, Subban was already one of the best offensive defensemen in the NHL. As the 2012–13 season started, he wanted Montreal to pay him what he thought he was worth. While talks went on between him and the team, the start of the NHL season was delayed by a **lockout**.

The season finally started in January 2013, but Subban missed Montreal's first few games. He still wanted a better contract. Once again some people criticized him. They thought he was too young to be asking for more money. And some players disliked Subban's style on the ice. In February 2013 *Sports Illustrated* said he was the most hated player in the league.

lockout—a period of time in which owners prevent players from reporting to their teams; owners do not pay players during lockouts and no games are played

FAST FACT

Subban signed a two-year contract with the Canadiens worth almost $6 million in 2013.

The personal attacks did not keep Subban from playing his best hockey ever. Because of the lockout, Subban played only 42 games. Still, he scored 11 goals and added 27 assists. His 38 total points tied for the most by an NHL defenseman that season.

One of Subban's best games of the season came in March against the New York Islanders. He scored on a slap shot in the second period and added another goal in the third in a 5-2 Canadiens win. The victory helped cement Montreal's division lead. The Canadiens finished the season as the top team in their division. But in the playoffs, they lost in the first round to the Ottawa Senators.

For Subban, though, the year was successful. He won the Norris Trophy, which goes to the league's best defenseman. He also was named to the All-Star Team for the first time. He had continued to prove he was one of the top players in the NHL.

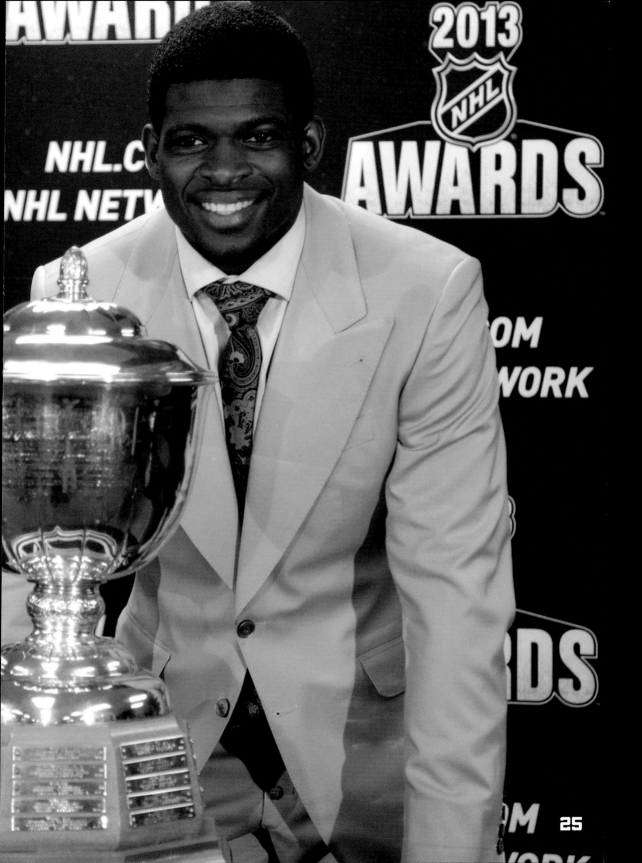

Subban talks with TV sportscasters during the 2013 NHL Stanley Cup Final.

While some hockey fans criticized Subban, many others praised and rooted for him. Along with showing amazing skills, he always played with great energy and seemed to enjoy himself on the ice. Away from the rink, he was comfortable being on TV and connecting with fans. He once appeared on *This Hour Has 22 Minutes*, a Canadian TV comedy show, and he established an active presence on Twitter. Some hockey experts thought Subban's exciting play and pleasing personality would attract more young fans to hockey.

Going into the 2013–14 season, many NHL players were thinking about the upcoming Winter Olympics. Subban made Canada's Olympic team, but he played in only one game. The team's coach Mike Babcock chose to use more experienced defensemen. Subban did not complain, and he won a gold medal as part of the team.

FAST FACT

Subban has called himself the Subbanator—a reference to the "Terminator" movies. He calls his fans Subbanation.

The end of the 2013–14 season saw Subban's amazing playoff performance. He led his team in scoring with 14 points in 17 games. The hockey world buzzed about his play. Then in late summer, Subban drew more attention when he signed a new contract with the Canadiens. Subban would earn $72 million over the next eight seasons.

By then Subban was not the only member of his family signed to an NHL team. His brothers, Malcolm and Jordan, had also been drafted. Someday they might be stars too. But for now, P.K. is the Subban who thrills hockey fans with his smart and energetic style of play.

P.K. Subban continued to amaze fans during the 2014–15 season. Canadiens fans were excited to see what the future held in store for their team and their superstar.

HELPING OUT

P.K. Subban knows not all kids have the same chance to play hockey that he did. That's why he and his family are involved with Hyundai Hockey Helpers. The organization raises money to help young Canadians buy hockey equipment and join leagues. "I wish a program like Hyundai Hockey Helpers was around when we were young. It's something we could have definitely benefited from," Subban said. "My father always taught us that sacrifice and practice make us better. Continued positive reinforcement has made my brothers and me the players we are today, and we're eager to pass on that message to those that may follow in our footsteps."

GLOSSARY

arrogance (AYR-uh-gants)—exaggerating one's own self worth or importance, often in an overbearing manner

blue line (BLOO LINE)—a line painted on the ice that marks the end of a team's offensive zone

defenseman (dih-FENS-muhn)—a player who lines up in a defensive zone to prevent opponents from getting open shots on goal

draft (DRAFT)—to choose a person to join a sports team organization or team

hat trick (HAT TRIK)—when a player scores three goals in one game

legacy (LEG-uh-see)—qualities and actions a person or team is remembered for

lockout (LOK-out)—a period of time in which owners prevent players from reporting to their teams; owners do not pay players during lockouts and no games are played

offense (AW-fenss)—the team that is in control of the puck and is trying to score

points (POYNTZ)—a player's total number of goals and assists

power play (POW-ur-PLAY)—when a team has a one- or two-player advantage because the other team has one or more players in the penalty box

racism (RAY-siz-uhm)—the belief that one race is better than others

rookie (RUK-ee)—a first-year player

slap shot (SLAP SHAHT)—the fastest and most forceful shot in the game; a player raises his or her stick and slaps the puck hard toward the goal, putting his or her full power behind it

Stanley Cup (STAN-lee KUP)—the trophy given each year to the NHL champion

veteran (VET-ur-uhn)—a longtime player

READ MORE

Gitlin, Marty. *The Stanley Cup: All About Pro Hockey's Biggest Event.* Sports Illustrated Kids: Winner Takes All. Mankato, Minn.: Capstone Press, 2013.

Stewart, Mark. *The Montreal Canadiens.* Team Spirit. Chicago: Norwood House Press, 2014.

Zweig, Eric. *Dominant Defensemen.* Hockey Hall of Fame Kids. Richmond Hill, Ontario: Firefly Books, 2014.

INTERNET SITES

FactHound offers a safe, fun way to find Internet sites related to this book. All of the sites on FactHound have been researched by our staff.

Here's all you do:

Visit *www.facthound.com*

Type in this code: 9781429691345

Super-cool stuff! Check out projects, games and lots more at
www.capstonekids.com

INDEX

American Hockey League, 14

Babcock, Mike, 27
Belleville Bulls, 10, 12
Boston Bruins, 5, 6, 7, 21

Calgary Flames, 19
Chicago Blackhawks, 21

Greater Toronto Hockey
    League, 10

Hamilton Bulldogs, 14
Hyundai Hockey Helpers, 29

Manitoba Moose, 14
Markham Islanders, 10
Markov, Andrei, 6
Minnesota Wild, 21
Montreal Canadiens, 5, 6, 7,
    12, 13, 14, 17, 19, 21, 22,
    24, 29

New York Islanders, 24
NHL lockout, 22
Norris Trophy, 24
North America, 18

Ontario Hockey League, 10
Orr, Bobby, 10
Ottawa Senators, 24

Philadelphia Flyers, 17
Pittsburgh Penguins, 17
President's Award, 14
Price, Carey, 6

Quebec, 13

Rask, Tuukka, 7
Rivet, Craig, 19

Sports Illustrated, 22
Stanley Cup, 13, 17
Subban, P.K.
    archer pose, 4, 19
    contracts, 22, 29
    facing criticism, 18–19,
        22, 26
    family, 8, 10, 12, 29
    first NHL games, 14
    first NHL goal, 17
    first NHL hat trick, 21
    named to NHL All-Rookie
        Team, 21
    named to NHL All-Star
        Team, 24
    nicknames, 27
    on Olympic team, 27
    on television, 26
    on Twitter, 26

*This Hour Has 22
    Minutes*, 26

U-20 World Junior Hockey
    Championship, 12–13

Washington Capitals, 17